Necessity

Necessity

Peter Sacks

W. W. NORTON & COMPANY

New York   London

For information about permission to reproduce selections from this book, write to Permissions,
W. W. Norton & Company, Inc., 500 Fifth Avenue, New York, NY 10110

The text of this book is composed in Bembo with the display set in Aperto
Composition by Adrian Kitzinger
Manufacturing by Courier Westford
Book design by JAM Design
Production manager: Julia Druskin

Library of Congress Cataloging-in-Publication Data
Sacks, Peter M.
Necessity / Peter Sacks.— 1st ed.
p. cm.
ISBN: 978-0-393-32504-1
I. Title.
PS3569.A235 N43 2002
811'.54—dc21   2002000319

W. W. Norton & Company, Inc., 500 Fifth Avenue, New York, N.Y. 10110
www.wwnorton.com

W. W. Norton & Company Ltd., Castle House, 75/76 Wells Street, London W1T 3QT

1 2 3 4 5 6 7 8 9 0

by no other way

CONTENTS

I.

15. V. 99 / 17

HEAD / 18

CRESTONE / 20

FLIGHT / 22

OFF THE FIELD / 24

THRESHOLD / 26

WINNOWING / 28

FLOOR / 30

DOVE / 32

NOTE / 35

II.

FACE TO FACE / 39

SERENADE / 40

WILDERNESS & THE AMERICAN MIND / 46

HORIZON / 48

THE TIME IT TAKES / 50

ABOVE THE FIRE / 52

28. XII. 99 / 54

EACH NEW ARRIVAL / 56

NOTE / 58

III.

FIRESTORM / 61

CURRENT / 62

BELOW THE FIRE / 63

WHAT WE SEE UNDER THE STARS / 64

UNDER THE SUN / 66

BOOK TWO / 69

THE UNGATHERING / 71

THE WORD / 73

IV.

VALEDICTION / 79

THORN / 80

RIVER (AS BEFORE) / 82

RIVER (TARGET) / 83

THIRD RIVER / 84

RIVER (FLARING) / 85

POSSIBLE RIVER / 86

RIVER (FIRE) / 87

SEVENTH RIVER / 88

THE SALIENT / 89

CITY / 90

V.

OCEAN / 95

Notes / 103

ACKNOWLEDGMENTS

Some of these poems first appeared in the following publications: *The Boston Review, The Colorado Review, Conjunctions, The Denver Quarterly, The Kenyon Review, The Yale Review.* "Head" first appeared in *Words for Images: A Gallery of Poems,* edited by John Hollander and Joanna Weber, Yale University Art Gallery.

Thanks to the Patrick Lannan Foundation for a residency during which parts of this book were written.

I

15. V. 99

Ravens more than twelve along the wire children shouting pointing up at one
so bright the flashing of *miraculous* was packed into the feathered sky & ocean

sapphire shoulder-cloak far denser than the jewels said to pave the stairway
to the upper fire black back feathers inter-faceted with glossy charcoal

indigo & violet then a momentary shaking-out & readjustment wings twice
    larger
than my hands outspread from interlocking thumbs the way we cast bird-
    shadows

on a wall as if it knew my likeness & unlikeness & the unnamed arrows
of amazement at the color & excess of what I took for joy or some wild
    under-

beauty throwing off its clothes down to the after-threads of light it turned
but not to face me this side of the wire why had I failed to see the bird

was trapped inside a shallow clock whose face was smeared with feathers
heart cut open & inset with numerals that took each other's place unheard

the beak crammed sideways to a perforation in the glass—air on my face &
on the faces of the children & within our lungs though I was barely
    breathing

& these words do not & thereby also have their portion of the truth.

HEAD

Simply to hold back the fraying stem, bud, scale, blur, wing, tooth,
eye-flecked water that will burn before the other signs give way,

earth-beaten, carved into the single root—your eyes now looking back
at my shelled sockets—shadow ships drowned out to carry their

own cargo stripped & hunted here—a search?—a harvest?—
wind comes over us unsung if not for other sounds—ancestral—

laboring—the memory of river-water—blades of quick attention
led away—that battleground you fasten over you—your skull, your face

of fiber hearing it if you can listen far enough—
there is a continent before the gods, there is a door of bone

between—behind you now the field is opening its jaws
below the ridge—there is no hollowness through which this whispering

can fall—no peace-filled re-imagining—now it is yours, repaid,
a monument through which no birdcalls seep—

you have to see it here, the place reserved for craft, for prayer,
in which you pause unknowing so these pieces of the tree—

not life, not replication—grow around us, thickening, however
much we cut them back, the branches of black ivory, the leaves

that open elsewhere to descend, ungatherable, around another generation's
thirst for everything between itself & its own end—do not

come home, they say, begin again, take all the time that's left, take Africa.

CRESTONE

A clearing before sunset & the westward-dropping slope ahead all but
invisible
                    flashed back from run-off underfoot.

I came down between pines & stands of wild
delphinium lit against pale aspen trunks & grass & new

buds cresting over tapered stems, chest high.

The earth's own shadow climbing through the trees toward

that nest of light up at the top,
                              until that too must go.

                    .

For what I cannot see, the words come later—

issuance, no door,
                    a rippled streak as of black lacquer-work

around the rim of what comes to the rendering of
itself.

What do you see on the already darkened surface

lipped in silver as it reappears within its track of vanishings?

And in that other glass

where mercury has flaked, whose skull?

What can you bring to it?

Self-ushering? Abstractions mass in you & scatter.

Are you already looking back?

FLIGHT

Far gone—another note?—in little starts, thin water
pushing forward over sand as if it too were listening

by grains, the furrow under film; it would be a relief,
that small correlative, it would be a continuance at dawn

when mountains bleed behind his eyes, & in the fault of night.

        ·

Of stone by stone by dint of glintings in the vein. And no
escape unless the braided murmurs can undo their silvering

between perception & the trickle of preliminary laws.

Ungathered, as for peace. And you can only follow,
pausing at a farther section of the wall.

        ·

What does it mean, here at the edge of thought
insisting on the slip & spillage—emergencies, self-hidden

lower leafage in the shadow of the ferns when there were ferns?

What does it want down there? Mint & stonecrop & thin
sapphire-colored dragonflies around the quarry?

Hovering; years later. Centuries. A little stiffer

in the neck. A seizure in the wind-shift near the rim.

.

The word for God is made inseparable from place—
drawn off & everywhere. No dust.

What does it leave but each thing ready & profane?
The sycamores shed scrolls of bark until they gleam,

a string of figures faltering around a knot where recognition
grips & tightens. Will it sink? Will it return now you have

entered & drawn near?

OFF THE FIELD

Pooling the resources of that morning's light he waited
until he too hung
                    unstirring in the understory while

the wind began to sort & shiver glossed bronze from
the ragged canopy.
                    White, molten, badges

at the verge of old extinguishings relit,
the sky

gone back to witnessing as if it were in greater need of
something rising

out—now audible, the ruffled sheen, & every layer scried
with opening—
                    the fence-lines tilted, snarled.

Unreasoning reflections? Tacit norms struck free?

So little time remains. The currents gather through

quick eddyings
                    accelerating past mere sharpenings, beyond

as yet unheard-of clarities that neither need nor want our

blood. Pine needles knit their shadows to the softened warp

of a still higher light

                   & it is wearable. No heart.

The years grow crammed, unchronicled.

The tracks are everywhere.

Come back out of the war, they say, come back.

THRESHOLD

The body quarreling, as if from inside it can know its place,

heat opening its mouth,
                     a rapid occupation, torn—

salt crusting in the aftermath.

Lower to the ground,
over remnants of bright mulch: the splintered fingerings,

the swallowed memory, sweet link, sweet fin,
glancing in the friction of the mist through which it moves.

Each mineral takes back its trace of blade & bone, of
first affiliation in the nib & ticking out.

If there is choice this is the lining under it,
unpierced.

If there is choice it strikes each particle that hangs

& spins in the near-weightless filament,
sweet whisper of electrum where the wheel must turn.

But soon only the ghost is visible between the trees;

& other ghosts already interpenetrate,
in seed, in through the needle's eye,

a little further off, a little throatless after-whistle

(*devoutly to be wished*) (the trickle

                            & the taint of it)—

& what they too had taken for (& taken back out of)
the hard residual innocence of life.

WINNOWING

Distances are changed above the water.
Flowing starts your crossing to the point

it knocks against you & there is no other.

Why is a word for the high wall. The waters rise.
Death a distant shuffle calls & calls

now taken up between the waters & the air.

                    .

You beat your hands against the burrowings,
the more than life-long sheath in which hard silts

have come to rest—(why now, the memory of harvesters
at night, their lanterns swinging over barley-sheaves?)—

a film of dust over your hands & feet, long sleeves of sand.

What unacknowledged love rides over you?

                    .

One counts the variations pouring
from that unintelligible source—
                              white pollen of the sea
dragged down to old instructions thickening the crest:

It's you, one sings into the surge.

And each frayed spirit entering

that anonymity.

FLOOR

As one who listens to the sequence alongside,
I built a fire. I went back to the line.

Earth, fence, wind—as one who listens to
the roots requiring more than rain,

more than a lamplit hand disturbing its own dust . . .

Between bone-meal & dirt I went. Trial paths
cut sideways in the course—

sap & vein—circulating tides—

"Fly where you are," one said, & then another.

        •

Shadows of pine needles ghost over the boards,

smoke-like, straying in & out,
counter-patterning the ripples of the grain.

The image searches its own origin across the screen
rehearsing figments of the uninhabitable

thread. The shuttle passes through.

        •

Weightless, soundless drift—
yet still perceptible caress,

     arousing passages of mind.

The branches dip & right themselves.

DOVE

The unpermitted (by the calling) grief so that face-down
through misery the point returns unsheathed,
                                    sensation under thought,
the light still early-blooded in this speed,
death turning inside out & you

learning to sing of it—cast out, not understoried,
                                    not filtering.

                    .

Listen: too many explanations of the will.
Where does it come from, meaning, till we say

full?
        The garden's taking off its mask.

Another, higher than the field, feasts there.

                    .

We wanted to go on, these were the wings.
No longer the near side of history.

The trees discovered their own need,
rebroken particles of soil & fire.

Near-dazzled in his island cave he spoke of peace

unsealed between him & the tide:

Do not pass by, he said.

And the leaves are for the healing of nations.

.

So it fell to
              what we might have heard had we been there—

the breeze under the light already shifting through the ranks,
the terms for peace redrawn between their opposites—blue, suturing,

sky-thread drawn loose or tight according to
the distant order of the imaging.

As one might say
              love we are in each other's keeping.

Having life, how measure it?

.

Still looking for the point of leverage, ground-level & in time.

No place outside relenting: no other way it could begin,

& then the dove: both calling out & drawing further in to the unseen.

Unsaving, saved, the silence changing under us.

What are you holding back? Light nested & was gone.

NOTE

Others choose more solid figures of resemblance but the wind
    blows from that place
dividing tissue seed flame unpermitted edges carrying the
    socket-bone's

implicit trial—here bend—here study it—the law remains torn
    feather scrap of
tarmac skin you fill it in you plough over the crater lip past
    argument the certain

flourish, short-stemmed, reachable with signaling what comes out
    of the wind
as an arrest, a feeding precedent, this rapid lifting now you link
    away drive out

each thrust upslope above the mark the mortar set you press
    against more weight
as for the future peace with gaps a hive a hull white shredding petal
    wave it will

not stop the work's upheaval where the impact shows its vein the
    unencompassable
paying out root thread survival-salted pollen knowing other
    judgment in the

sideways trace & drag you cast you follow it.

II

FACE TO FACE

The sky too fed upon itself
                    & hid behind the point where everything takes on
the sheen of disbelief.
Justice shivered in its mask.

The residue of innocence would speak if it had words. Would cry out

once more for what name? What is its sin, there at the origin?

SERENADE

Clean it up, the god says.

We tie the snakes into a ring.
We beat stones together.

Cleaner, says the god.

We roll the surface back.

Light grows solid in our arms.

        ·

God says, no god, no fingerprint.
No mule standing in a cloud
of flies. You want to

set it down, the
hit & miss of numbers
cut along the fence,

the banjo grown back
into the shoulders,
rank & file.

Harm's way, harm's worth.
After the drought the small
blue flowers shiver on the dunes.

.

Elsewhere you

say mine say stranger
stronger break
dirt breath first

laws
stone scroll
fire calling

eat here choke this
unburned

honey down

o wilderness.

.

Once I got soaked
said yes front
yes back sky

filed down
no money made it
come so hurried

sounds like
justice all-
at-once

& fish out
swimming in it.

                    .

Crowd of rags blown out along the road. Eradicated flight
if you could call it that. And stiff-necked, stooping

to each share, a closing motion, dust nailed through.
A trap, iron teeth sunk into bone.

Wind, work, mockery—
a ribbon of stiff dirt laid to one side where hardpan broke.

The racket clatters on. The god terms change. The images of mind.

                    .

I broke the padlock, used a shovel on the door. You could feed a horse on what
had grown up through the boards. Sluice-box, rusted screen; a gray rag on a
chair. The nails were glistening. Starshift, flint & iron brought near, until I
moved again. Get back, I said, you & your prison song.

                    .

Who'll toss the boy a coin? This far

---

from where we should have given up—

thunder & a hundred miles
of uncut grasses swaying in the memory of rain.

And in this road, no fork.
The desert standing like a wall on fire.

That sound of water, where's it coming from?

Who'll toss the boy a coin?
Otherwise we have to make it up,

judges looking down like rain-
clouds under oath.

They wear you down.
Where's the background? Why isn't there a background

sound? Where is it coming from?
A blade? A single blade? We're asking you

before you leave, before we sew you shut.

                    .

That night the fox screamed & we called it peace.

He'd always had a tortured way of speaking,

beautiful but tortured.

Smoke?

So little time:

Thrown up, the cities seethe.

See here he said, the furrows are
obedient:

you plough, you scrape away, you drag it out.

One leans upon a gate,

the other sings into a corridor of meat.

        .

But that was afterwards,
a line of dry blood on the knife.

From the start it was
my nickel, your scenario.

Chewing the familiar
fragrances.

That's when the lid came off? We woke?

Just how to carry on out here?

You said the world was of an age & we were following
a swirl of notes, of *tones,* of what comes

naturally into confusion & remains.

But that was afterwards.

Such freedom, such long afternoons.

WILDERNESS & THE AMERICAN MIND

What is the structure of a curse?

Some murmured *revolution* & you saw it there—

blood on the road in place of
knowing. Then

knowing for sure.

                    .

The ancestors have never been more agitated,
arms & legs hung out to dry, fingers

testing surface tension on the mounds.

Fearful, covetous
we made our way across.

Some gates swung open

& we broke the others down.

                    .

The land to body ratio; you can't have both
we said before the wind took hold.

Afraid to hurt, afraid to suffer more—

what would it mean to stay alive?

.

I could have sworn there was a map—

Soon after we arrived
I read the stories of true

heartlessness—

too simple to have said they had nowhere to go.

New forms of poverty, a show of force

(why should the tongue swell up that way?)

The kid rebuilt the fire with bones.

We paid him out in kind.

HORIZON

Beginning with the
heart as with

the other
carcasses

I stretched it
out to dry.

The river swung
through depths of

its own time-lapse

under rain wind
cloudlight

bodying
necessity—

no entrance
but to break what

wraps around &
over us.

We might have
worn it

as a wing,
sight-lines quickening a

net so there is
death enough

brought near
re-faceting

indented

kindling.

It tugs at us,
the clench & suction

tightening for more.

THE TIME IT TAKES

The dead are in one place.
                    Dry heat, the mouth turned inside out.

As one might say the words (& in the time it takes)
the ghosts pass through each other to the power of dust.

Thorn-tree, a cloud, then nothing hung behind the flat crown of the tree.

Above cracked stone & sand he recollects
                              clear river-water

entering a mountain pool, the swirl of current
rippling its lens over a slope of

weed, sand, dimmer waters where
the eye sinks into stillness till it pulls away.

As others stand behind a proper name
he recollects the peace in which men think of war.

They pass. A phrase, a feathering of air.

Would they still hack away the children for a sign?

Though he is silent, writing it, the children
stand in line.

At that remove

the argument depends on what I cannot call to witness.

Now they file past.

These are my hands.

ABOVE THE FIRE

Above the fire a man floats in a boat.

Above the fire a woman is devoured by a snake,
                                        unseen.

The leaves are yellow alongside & in the wake

the trunks & branches
mirror one another, black, rain-soaked.

And now he's old. He trails a hand until it snares
a leaf—saw-toothed.

Clouds break above the buildings
where there had been none.

The snake is old, its jaw competely
unhinged for the swallowing.

What now?

There was a continent.

Below, the last gods burn along with their last
offerings—

no smoke, no film, no evidence.

The gold-shagged blizzard of the willow

spills again.

Climb down. Prevent.

He leans back & the oar drips like no other memory.

28. XII. 99

Makeshift it follows
instantly & to

the west
you say it's not

familiar
this brief half-

frozen section of
river, yes—

believable
by choice by

these brown
doves low down along

the edge all
motionless

not yet
alarmed, not

wickering off—

the famished
way oblivion

won't back off—

we always could have

asked for further
proof. America.

EACH NEW ARRIVAL

One nation under god vestigial & aroused.
I wanted power, power wanted blood—

only our bodies left between us & the path bewildering
its last particulars.

The windows darken & the air is darkened water.
Call it the wind but is it?

.

At their own intervals the bells swing bronze into this smoldering
through which we enter separate cities built of cruelty.

And it is all still killable.
The sun drops off.

The soil turns over in the shadow of itself.

.

You wonder with what kind of mind. Outside (outside) a dragonfly. Blue spindle, living
thread, piece of the chariot according to the river (ours) laid open to clear water trembling
where the wings slice through.

.

Tell the others not to wait.
Love rises out of time. A mound of raw meat freezing to the sled.

Fire spreads through flesh cloth plaster tearing off for miles—

the last two faces of necessity becoming one—the sun,
the intersecting thorn.
                    There'd been a city, & another phrase
(*torched honeycomb*) in which we saw the last inhuman shape love made

of us—*No other resting place,* the armless figure says.
Next time you'll die for it again.

NOTE

Had you existed (this world) had you set your own equivalent
    across the track
would there have been a further purpose clearing the debris? Or
    earlier—before

the call, before the guarantees (the stars of heaven, sand, the wings
    resettling
above ordinary slaughters)—was it to frighten us away? How
    solitary,

with smoke mixed in, with scrapings. Listen—let the others hear
    the long
collisions wrapped in silence. Blank flag of surrender & no writing
    covers you.

FIRESTORM

There was a hand he said, & held it up.

.

Unburied stacked
this must have been

the clearing,

birds sing & the air
resettles its

divisions.

.

Go.

See how the berries shine.

CURRENT

The fossil of the fish in candlelight—a dorsal fin
set wavering by current & the spine more flame than stone.

Breathe in.
The words too grow transparent, heard-through, to this end.

What's nearest to you now?
Ungathered sediment, you're swaying on your stem

time loosens, thins, through-lit as by an older
element.
          It knows you as you will become.

BELOW THE FIRE

As dead leaves in the space between leaf-shadows gleam, he could not
keep from waking further, disentangled from what might have been

perpetual fear. The core takes longer—first whom, then what.

As if all flesh were punishable proof.

They had been everywhere, the trees.

WHAT WE SEE UNDER THE STARS

She leaned down from the riverbank

He was explaining why he loved & there could be no better reason.

This became one limit.

What remained was late but more immediate.

Her face bent nearer.

Then the flames dodged & their shadows merged & swam like
    water on the wall.

       .

Still laying claim to.

Living-space
a mouth far down under the leaves.

They carved their hands into the door.

       .

Because my mind lay in the path the wheel
crushed it here against the riverbed.

There was a pool, we bathed, there had been trees.

So reaching up, my left hand guiding & the right below
the shaft.

These are the clouds.

                    .

Bones of the never-brother. Of the wolf.

As one looks in a well
he knew where his life's blood had been.

If I still had a throat I'd drink the wind.

UNDER THE SUN

You move the chair aside.

You touch yourself, accordingly.

Your wrist; a piece of driftwood; iron
where there was nothing.

Meaning it.

.

Blunt positings along the edge of need
withheld.

.

We're not the wind.

.

No inhuman mercy.

.

Uneven suck-back of clear spillage on a tray of stones.

No trail, no beach.

The resolution fell apart.
The crop was in—that nest of wire—

the gathered genius bled face-down into the sand.

　　　　　·

No figurehead looked out to where the view explodes.

Relabelled. Wrapped in flags.

To make one thing—
song & its opposite under the flares.

One song.

　　　　　·

I prayed for it, appraising every hook,

the counter solid with what used to be

authority—grease of interest where

the meal had been prepared—

O *little town*—the repetition of the pulp
until your arms caught fire.

　　　　　·

The ramps pulled up knee high.

Iron filings auctioned off the knives.

                    .

Because we have gone through
(to speak of it inside but look away)

Because we are still willing

Because we thicken speech until it tears at us

(thick rim-blocks, veering bell)

Because the balance sinks

(clawed deep into what feeds itself)

Because there is no other who can kneel
Because there is no other who can bring the axe-head down

You move the chair aside

You touch yourself accordingly.

BOOK TWO

The more
we are the lost

belief I

see your hands
you listen

through the mind's
bright crash & drag of

fluency
you have been

leaping by example—leaf

flame muscle bell where

meaning has its
mound still singing

torchlight slithers over

silt the limestone

city bedded
over us each voice

bends to its own

supply we

reach
& turning fall

we fall.

THE UNGATHERING

By choice
I never heard

the scraps

in one night . . .

*fell from
Purgatory,*

tarmac
cracked unruly

inward
parts—to save

both mindful
& desiring

resurrection without
dying

*then with
dying—*

star-root
bone-root

chewing,

not to be released

this altered
air the unconfined

now entering the
late arrivals who

already listen
from the far

side slipping

their own senses
only through this

certain
taking-its-

unending-
measure-of

resistance

(shape &
counter-shape)

exchanged

(open the window love again).

THE WORD

I.

The word was never *mercy*
or the future never would have sung of it.

—

Black fin
horizon-milled nicks flickering.

—

Fresh wet, & the alarm
chewed off.

The shatterable structure seething:

if we'd time, if we
could cross another field.

—

What sorrowful augmenting
in the face of

scarcity?

—

Dug in, do they re-use

the focus,

—

given work?

II.

If in their desire they acted,

their action aimed at what they craved—

& that was vision, & an object of vision.

—

Speed of

(down-
shifting

brokered)

those are scales
from under

brighter than
reflections

welded mouthing

limitless but for
the world we

push ourselves
from braced

& it said

take them both.

IV

VALEDICTION

Here, drink—enough to spill a little in the dust—kind

history—the daylight lying back unbreathing in its force,
& little warning left, the final spiral vine fleece feather

floating up, bright filigree of leaf around the law. Take off
the slab of leather smoke grease smear of lime under *my people*

swung through earth the centuries still cling to, cortex blade & shield—
shear back—more than your single life, cupped up & beaten out like this.

                    •

We gather further off. We build.
Old candle-stumps held up, they stand me on a box, the claw-shaped

pointer in my hand, the soul lifted past each character until it
warms its hands above the glowing rags

necessity is hunching through, reclotting, fixed stars going off—(for hope
read *image of,* read *breaking up to where new silhouettes stand up*

against the glow, admonishing)—seep-willow desert-willow spun-
beneath-the-untouched-portion-willow

& nothing equal to the sound of high tide shattering the stone sea wall.

THORN

A woman takes her clothes off in the flames. What do they mean by
    majesty
without the weapon just ahead of time? I pocketed this green-black
    stone out of a

thousand hills. No face. About the weight of my hand in my hand.

Where tracks had been, ice crystals scrape the glass like salt but higher-
    pitched. Returning here
equipped (*a man with two stripes is a corporal*) until it shines. Until the
    rifling makes the bullet spin.

Would you have wept, so premature, so much a side-effect?

What *is* the miracle at twilight on the seventh day (so cold)?

We say it's fear that shapes the unapportionable burning back we took
    for sky.

.

What does it imitate, the knife? The ear is delicate. The laws of sight are
    born where you
break surface.

The wind is here in spirit & hospitable. Two single-noted birds take turns
    re-piecing what might
otherwise be further emptied out. My face-net

open for inspection, spade-shaft levering, surplus of unfrozen dusk, white
   door into the earth's
inconstant knot of bare stems hard to make out underfoot.

Beneath thick quickenings you enter freely, so mutable. The shock & glut
   crowd up then ebb.
As unevading others will, you will.

RIVER (AS BEFORE)

          As before.

The interlocking spirals of analogy
flash through the crust,

             half-willed unsteady vanishings—it was a war
of our continuing—tribes caught between the brickyard & the dunes—

there will have been a wall—
of kings—of ships against the inland sea—the figureheads gone back

to broken spray. Look down between dry crests & hand-shaped
edges of the weeds.

Of blame. And others praising.

RIVER (TARGET)

Splitting the high reeds, the net of sound sinks through a mesh of
    moving lights & disappears.

Silicates one thousandth of a millimeter thick bind & flicker in
    the ditch. Of oscillations,

not yet fear.
            Shoals sleep & stir, unscarce, the birdcries over them.

Wild sweetness. Breeze. The dint & irrigating quick to turn aside . . .

Is it oblivion along the bank, the spirit filtered out, afloat, inaudible?

Was there a garden planted with the leaves unmarked,
was there a garden here, not yet for healing?

                        How else to live outside?

Ashes too are in the words for it—stem, petal, shadowed edge
between us, gathering, print of cinder in the sunlight

saying *choose*—repeating *needle's eye.*

THIRD RIVER

There is another element: the limbs laid out & carried burning

without harm, so wanted, so drawn-out,
entangled drifts will not give way as much as wrap the passage—

finger-spindles tearing at the hem.

Thick braids sweep out to where the bright inhuman gaze will
rest exchanged, then scatter over us.
                                    One calls & calls
sideways, gathering as much as he can hold—gray-blue clay already

hardening around the straw marked off & fed into the fire.

And other cities where the living wait.

RIVER (FLARING)

How would you *know*? Then repetitions tried for other tones—no, *thorns*—
cut down or ripped from where they'd

hung. I'd gone along (as for the remnant), blue-black reddening out
then white under the sound of salt.

Was there a camp nearby (as for the ritual), was there a fence?

Only the idiot flaring up in stripes.

Only the long god of the hours slithering.

POSSIBLE RIVER

The rhythms vary, spectral but enchained to their own opposites—
bedrock & hidden boulder, skirmishes left wriggling in the

friction of light wind. *If, if* . . . the new condition laying bare
what you can make of it—

a line of starlight possible however ripped—you
bend & drink the image till your palm is dry.

RIVER (FIRE)

> ... so-carved, as winter

entering the sieve behind each branch now rinses later paler will not
drown the sediment of root-work choir-work—your own chain

of breath first shaken back from its last link laid open,

unshelled pulse-note shingled sedged you too left out along
the path.

The water gives its own equivalent,
slipping its own sheath as it goes on.

The cross-wires tremble.
Mouth of shade.

The whole length of the sword & sword-arm blaze at once.

SEVENTH RIVER

The memory of sunflowers open to the wind then burning.

Cedar-shadow then a thought of shade.

Each moment less than my own body's length
from where the air says it is not

release from passion but return to the high
waters shadowing the ark.

Death is the room.

Law is the revelation of the law,

as it is said of animals:

to enter into the water to drink of it.

THE SALIENT

Until it came—transparent lark & lurk, slow purpose—toward his
    backing off,

black fin swaying over green weed-elongated hands,

the single bell rung, towering & relenting, giving out.

           .

All day birds floated on the membrane. Sunlight crossed & lost itself by
    scraps, the table tilted, sank.
Whoever sleeps here wakes to nothing but long shadows on the shifting blind.

Be still, this undisplayed wing leaves you undistracted by the last flesh-colored
    wall between us &
the stump of what had been the whole.

Spade's dry skin scraping off the lining where we listen under guard.

Then all at once onshore, shot down, dying off per yard. *If you* . . .

More names cut deep into the only space. As once. In time of war. If you
    should pray.

CITY

What happened to the trench? Blood-flies—writing with her lips against
  the wall.

And streaming fern-like particles at dawn: *in truth, I have come through the*
  shuttered wavering

my hair is wet with it. The wing works over surface hunger—probing—

Let me bury you.

Enough to make you bend between the two stone arms.

What are the other facts? The birdcalls kill each morsel of new silence
  heard too late.
In droves, in dark blue clods below the overseer & his horse—

the stirrups silvering to where the field will end.

                    .

What will have passed for vision in the border-zone?
Between appearances, striped stones set upright in the riverbed.

Long scrolls unravel.
He waits, you wait, we wait.

The candle takes to pulsing in its jar & everything grows jittery against
  the shade.

Part whole. Blank immolation of the wick. Each fragment drafted doubling.
Why look back at the sky?

•

Is there no other door unframed by death & by the dead who hear the sound
   of heaven coming to its end? Brought near then tightening.

What can be built? The balance levels on the watermark.
The weapons lean in shadow on the wall. But for memory: the rising skyline

every purpose has prepared. I will have sung of it. You sing. Who else will
   turn the high blue pages back to their critique of sadness?

Listen: the massive petals open now,

here, here in the inward parts.

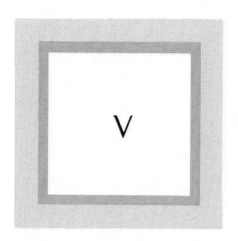

V

OCEAN

I left my face up there & went on with the others over stones weed sand
     blurred
tree-trunk hull bridge factory walls now darkening the bed, the mouths
     of pipes

old jetty stumps & pylons, green, moss-purple, shredded outlets lengthening
the drag where there could be (remade) a body. Cities climbed high-throated

toward others listening if they were not at war.

———

Distinctions ripped, the haul of meat & bone—fish scouring
proper names for One, cut deep, the point of (human)

purchase, fulcrum, leveling. Aching joints. White scales.

So that we bent down lifting it to save or sell again.

———

There is a principle, intact & yours to hold, remember?

Back-light dips, prismatic, faltering by length, by speed of its descent
sharpened *stone by stone.*
                         Even the sound will change its own

insistence, stronger than the wincing wind in higher places of the field:

If you could concentrate, if you could gather every prior gift.

Now can you number them, the mouths held open as for rain, not
    shadowing?

———

And others led away in lines—what can you set aside here for the
    messenger of parts,
given the scarcity (given freedom),

more than the particle you grazed unseeing as you fell?

Blue shoulder, arm; the whole wave shattering the rush of doors.

———

Cast out by interval—grip & release—the casing of hard light
around each head, no helmets reddening, the eyes gone through

to mineral & winter.

                    Then it comes again—a fold, a reach of seed
hurled downslope pouring its stored purposes between

each shock wave & ourselves slit open, thrown by one who knows,

who watches every act—the burrowing, the torturing, the
screaming at the wall—who hears what would be spoken in despair

if we should speak.

———

And always this one carried on a short spike.
Always more who cannot turn the storm away.

Red in the field & in the face. Ice-blue.

"I am the origin" (the beggar's spine beneath your hands) (the only edge).

"I know. I am the wind."

———

And so it was, such history
by night when others bear it off, worm-song & ant.

Come back now that you're hacking down the tree. How are you spending it?
Why else be terrified?

———

See how it smudges, how it's literal?
So quick, another's youth, another era's.

Swallow-tail on fire. Rafters feathering. You
    still staring,

embers in your eyes when you had eyes.

———

First virtues blistering the law.

Strapped down, then iron clamps, lord

(fixity above all else), unto the highest ranks who watch,
who can afford to watch

so those who cry out in the name of ritual, regime of
shoulder-bones gnawed off above a waste of words

(sweet treaty, guide me home),

potholes of reddened tar . . .

———

The strong god, ignorance, holds up the vapor trail
between us & our fate. To make it fair.

And was it memory on fire, the mother flailing outward crushed
into oblivion so-called.

And every future sun rising at once.

———

In spite of it, you count the bones, I sing of other harmonies,

the centuries buckle into sleep,

no other witnesses, salt everywhere.

These are the tears of children, & the surface swallows them.

——

What do you have to trade? What would you die for
this far in the track?

I'm asking every rut & furrow,
messenger.

——

"If one compares the world of Forms to a living, variegated sphere,
or to something made up only of faces . . . one would see it, but as it were
from the outside, as one being sees another. In fact, however, one must
oneself become Spirit, and oneself become vision." —Plotinus.

Letting the figure bleed:

"We are like faces turned toward the outside, but attached on the inside to
one single head."

——

You've seen them peel back the momentary
cover,

mouthing names for god

(As if. As such.)

The whole sky chewing its own tongue.

———

What of the unfurling rose, four outer petals set against the light
as yet unshadowed by the inside flower, the rim transparent, coraline,

already turning back toward the hardened calyx under it—

Do not, it opens further, *Do not.* Weighing everything:

———

And other flowers, other syllables.
The air moved, pale-mouthed.

The crease of exile, I once called it.

———

You must, you must (the god again), blunt fingers in the wine,

uncounted dolphins caught & strangled in the net.

———

A wet snow on the shore at dusk.

(Astride.) The afterlife of slaves.

———

When I set out I thought of justice.
It was cold & fair. It was the color of consent,

more shapely than a flower, or the sky forever

opening as we turn, self-balancing.

There were trees along the shore,
quick water-lights glanced up & climbed the leaves

till there were none. . . .

Even the poor grew ashen on the inside.
Even the poor let go the sad investigations.

One step away from nakedness on either side,
I walked on, following my version of the first blade

cutting in this far,
so that another voice could drop between the words.

Return, blind one. You. Blinded one.

NOTES

"Dove." The phrase "And the leaves are for the healing of nations," is adapted from *Revelations* XXII.2.

"The Word." The first three lines of section II are adapted from a phrase of Plotinus, *Enneads* III.8.